Flying Toys

MILNER CRAFT SERIES

Flying Toys

A GREEN HOBBY THAT'S LOTS OF FUN

KENNETH SAMS

SALLY MILNER PUBLISHING

First published in 1991 by
Sally Milner Publishing Pty Ltd
67 Glassop Street
Birchgrove NSW 2041 Australia

Reprinted in 1992

© Kenneth Sams, 1991

Production by Sylvana Scannapiego,
Island Graphics
Cover design by Gatya Kelly, Doric Order
Illustrations by Kate Edwards and Gatya Kelly
Typeset in Australia by Asset Typesetting Pty Ltd
Printed in Australia by Impact Printing, Melbourne

National Library of Australia
Cataloguing-in-Publication data:

Sams, Ken.
    Flying toys.

    ISBN 1 86351 038 9.

    1. Kites. I. Title.

795.15

The author, Kenneth Sams, has been
flying and developing these fabulous
flying toys for many years, and refers to
them as Unconventional Flying Objects
or UFOs, and this is what they are
called throughout the book.

Contents

Preface

UFOs are Unconventional Flying Objects. Nothing like them has ever flown before. In this book I hope to share with you the great pleasure the UFO has brought me during the past ten years.

UFOs are easy to make and they're even easier to fly. The materials you need are cheap and available in local shops.

In this book are basic designs for the UFOs. Some will be gliders. Some will be tethered. Some will fly hundreds of metres high. Some will be small and weigh less than a few grams. Some might be big enough to lift you off the ground.

▶ LEGAL CAUTIONS

My UFO designs are copyright and patented worldwide. No one is allowed to make them for sale or profit without my permission.

▶ ACKNOWLEDGEMENTS

This book could not have been completed without the excellent support and assistance I received from Margaret Sams, Gregory Sams, Diane Blackwell, and Nigel Wilson.

UFO Gliders

▶ MAKING A BASIC UFO GLIDER

The best way to explain the UFO is to take you through the same steps I went through to invent it. All you need is a ruler, a piece of paper, scissors and sticky tape.

Cut out a rectangle 3cm x 12cm (1¼″ x 4¾″) from a sheet of firm but light paper.

Throw the paper in the air as high as you can. Note how it starts spinning and goes into a glide rather than falling straight to the ground.

Fold it 2cm (¾″) from each end, so it looks like this.

Throw it in the air again. Notice how it comes down in a straighter glide than when unfolded.

What made the difference? The bit of paper we folded vertically on each end offered stability.

Lay two of these shapes on top of each other with all their vertical folded ends sticking up and seal them together where they touch. You can seal with a bit of sticky tape where the folded ends meet. Alternatively you can staple them together, or use glue or paste.

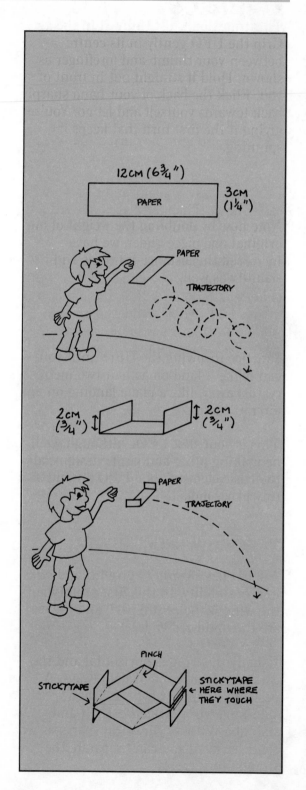

After they're stuck together, pull the two pieces of paper apart in the centre, opening them up.

This time don't just throw it in the air. Grip the UFO gently in its centre between your thumb and forefinger as shown. Hold it straight out in front of you. Flick the back of your hand sharply back towards yourself and let go. You're giving it the first turn that keeps it spinning.

Note how by doubling the weight of our original one piece glider, we have increased the distance it travels and its stability as well.

Practice throwing the UFO until you can make it land on a chair two metres (yards) away, like a plane landing on an aircraft carrier.

This is your first UFO. Although we'll be making other and larger designs, all the basic elements of a UFO are in this tiny paper model.

A UFO has a *wing* to give lift and *ears* to give stability. In this first prototype, the wing is the centre part, and the ears are the upturned ends.

Usually the wing is horizontal and the ears are vertical … but not always. A perfectly cylindrical shape, when spinning, will provide *both* lift and stability. With a cylindrical shape, as we shall see later, you can't separate the wing from the ears.

3

▶ A BIGGER UFO GLIDER

Now let's go beyond the paper stage to make big gliders that will fly six metres (20′) across your living room, giving you enough time to walk across and catch them before they touch down.

For the best results buy some waterproof florists' ribbon (the ribbon must be of a rigid enough texture to retain its shape). From a roll of ribbon you can make many UFO gliders.

If you can't get ribbon use heavier paper or plastic film or even those foam plastic cartons you get in takeaways. Make the design bigger. For example, using the same paper we used for the 12cm (4¾″) model, cut out two pieces 6cm x 22cm (2¼″ x 8½″) and staple or tape them together 4cm (1½″) from each end. (A stapler will prove very useful. It saves messing around with sticky tape.)

Because UFOs made of waterproof florists' ribbon are the most successful, the instructions for later glider models will include dimensions for that ribbon.

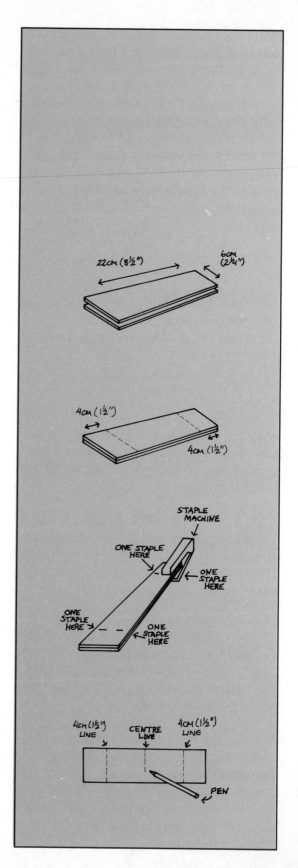

4

However, paper can still be used. There will be times when you'll have to make the paper models smaller than the ribbon models. But after a while, you'll be able to judge the size that retains enough rigidity to spin.

There's a lot of tolerance in the dimensions I give in these instructions. Just being close is usually good enough.

Fold back the ends of the wings outside the staples to form ears.

If you used the florists' ribbon, your UFO glider will weigh very little indeed.

Later on, we'll be putting rods (axles) through these designs and launching them into tethered flight. But there's so much fun you can have with UFO gliders, let's stay with them a while.

▶ **FLYING YOUR UFO**

First, practice launching it so it goes where you want it. Remember, thumb and forefinger grip it gently in the centre, back of hand flips back towards you from the wrist, and you release the UFO glider, giving it the first spin.

You know you have the knack of launching when every time you flip it, it goes where you want it to go. It takes a little practice!

- Try to land on a chair 6 metres (20′) away.

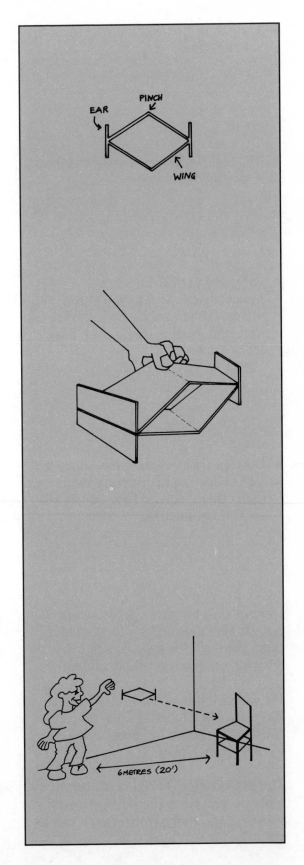

5

- Launch it, then walk alongside it and catch it again.

- Stand at the top of a stairway and let it glide slowly down.

- After you get the knack, get somebody else to face you three metres (10') away. Launch the UFO back and forth to each other. Play UFO catch.

- Develop the game by each taking a UFO glider and launching them at each other. You can have two in the air at the same time.

As your skill improves, give each person two UFO gliders and try to keep four of them going all the time. It's not that difficult, once you get the hang of it.

It's surprising how few mid-air collisions there are when four UFOs are constantly passing in opposite directions in this limited airspace.

You can play UFO catch with three or more people. Keep the UFO gliders spinning and flying from one person to the other.

- Another fun UFO game if you don't have a partner is UFO bounce. Face a wall two metres (6') away and launch your UFO against the wall. If you hit the wall high enough, the UFO will reverse and come back to your hands. See how many times you can make it come back.

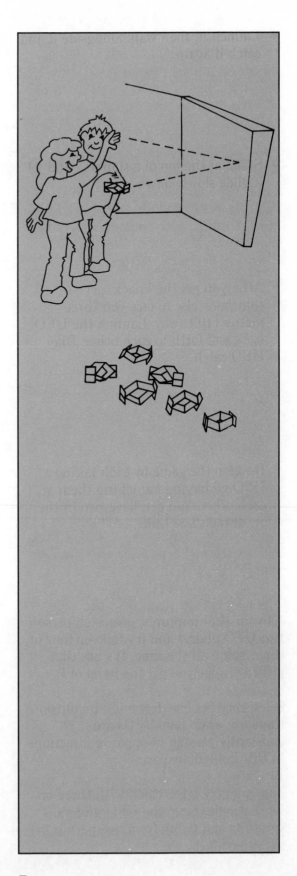

- Make a dozen or so UFO gliders. It's always good to have a stock on hand.

- I enjoy just walking up and down my room, playing catch with my UFO glider. Flip the UFO from one end of a six metre (20') long room and then walk slowly behind it, as it spins in front of you. Catch it just before it lands and send it back across the room again. It's a great excuse for indoor walking exercise.

- Fly the UFO glider outside when the wind is light. Stand at a window or on a porch and drop it down into the garden or street. It will sometimes perform like a bubble, catching those subtle wind currents around houses. I've had them rise over rooftops after catching an updraft.

If you launch a UFO glider from a great height, say the roof of a tall building, there's no telling how far it will travel before it touches down. You'll discover all sorts of interesting things about air currents.

You can even drop fifty or more together out of a cardboard box from a height, to make a spectacular display. Each UFO takes a separate path to the ground and the air is filled with them as they very slowly spin their way to the ground. (You will, of course, retrieve them.)

▷ *UFO Tennis*

And now for a real fun UFO glider game — UFO tennis. Any kind of stick will do as a racket and the UFO is your ball.

The name of the game is to keep the UFO glider constantly spinning. Launch it then catch it with the tip of your stick before it hits the ground. Lift it up as high as you can with the stick and release it. Repeat. The trick is to catch the glider with the stick right in the very centre so that it doesn't fall off when you raise it.

When you get the hang of it, you'll be able to guide the UFO's direction with your wand. And if you're really good, you'll be able to keep two or more UFOs spinning all the time.

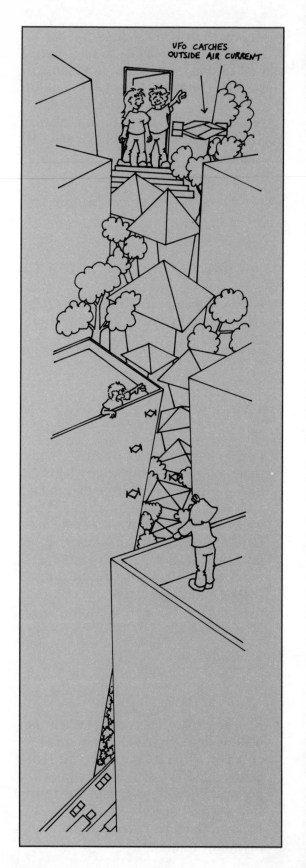

UFO CATCHES OUTSIDE AIR CURRENT

8

▶ LARGER SIZE UFO GLIDERS

Make larger 7cm x 26cm (2¾″ x 10½″) UFO gliders. Use two staples on each side to bind them together. Staple 6cm (2¼″) in from each end.

If you scale up dimensions to go beyond this size you'll need sturdier material.

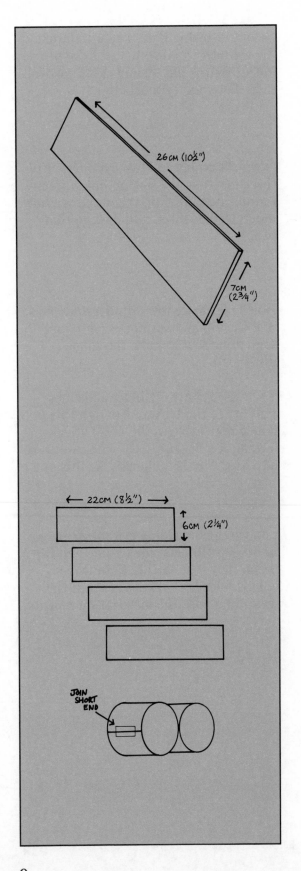

26CM (10½″)

7CM (2¾″)

▶ CYLINDRICAL UFOs

Cylindrical UFO shapes also perform well as gliders and they offer a wide range of design possibilities.

To make one, cut out four pieces 6cm x 22cm (2¼″ x 8½″).

Take one piece. Join its short ends together using sticky tape, staples or glue. (Just like making paper chains!)

Throw this cylinder in the air. Note how its fall, though steep, is stable.

Now make another cylinder and sticky tape, staple or glue the two cylinders together.

Flip your 2-cylinder model in the air. Note how it travels considerably farther than one on its own.

To make a spinning thing fly better you can increase its weight but the added weight must be placed in the right place.

← 22CM (8½″) →

6CM (2¼″)

JOIN SHORT END

Before throwing it aloft again, flatten the cylinders a bit so that they're no longer round, but oblong. See how well these flattened cylinders fly.

Now let's go beyond two cylinders. Put three together, not oblong but perfectly round this time. Flip them and see how much farther three cylinders go than two.

Now take the centre cylinder and crease it at the top and bottom, so you have something looking like the shape illustrated.

The raised centre cylinder adds more stability to the UFO. Although this is not so noticeable in the UFO glider format, it will show itself when we start tethering UFOs designed like this one.

Can you go on adding cylinders? If you fix seven cylinders side by side and flip them, they'll go farther than three. A ten cylinder UFO glider is about the maximum with the material we're using.

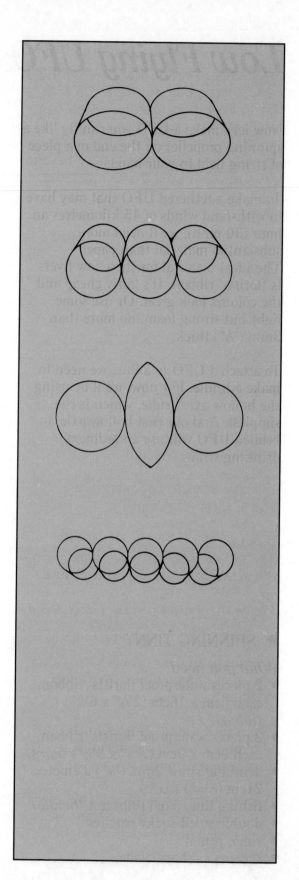

Low Flying UFOs

Now let's make a UFO you can fly like a spinning propeller on the end of a piece of string held in your hand.

To make a tethered UFO that may have to withstand winds of 45 kilometres an hour (30 mph), we'll need more substantial material than paper.
The ideal material for these low flyers is florists' ribbon. It's fairly cheap and the colours look great. Or use some light but strong foam, no more than 3mm (1/8″) thick.

To attach a UFO to a line, we need to make a bridle. For now, we'll be using the hollow axle bridle, which is the simplest. And our first hollow axle bridled UFO will use an ordinary drinking straw.

▶ SPINNING TINNY

What you need:
- 2 pieces waterproof florists' ribbon, each 6cm x 16cm (2¼″ x 6¼″) *(wing)*
- 2 pieces waterproof florists' ribbon, each 6cm x 9cm (2¼″ x 3½″) *(ears)*
- drinking straw 3mm (1/8″) diameter, 21cm (8¼″) *(axle)*
- fishing line, 5kg (10lb) test *(bridle)*
- double-sided sticky patches
- ruler, pencil
- scissors or sharp blade

Take a wing piece and put a sticky patch on each corner. Make sure half of each patch projects so it can grip the other wing piece.

Remove the protective covers from the sticky patches.

Make the two wing pieces into one cylindrical piece by touching their ends together so the sticky patches grip them. You still have one side of each sticky exposed.

Take the ear pieces and lay them against the exposed sticky. Make sure they're centred. Now what you have should look like the diagram.

Cut the corners off each ear so they look like this.

Using the pointed end of scissors or a ballpoint pen or, best of all, a hole puncher, punch a hole through the exact centre of each ear. This is where the straw axle goes.

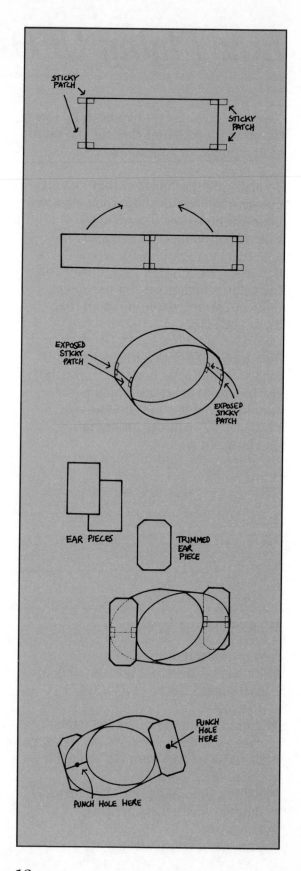

Take the 21cm (8¼″) long drinking straw and cut off 5mm (¼″) pieces from each end. Save these pieces. You'll need them later.

To strengthen the open ends of the straw, barely touch the flame of a match to it so it just starts to melt. Just barely, or it will distort.

Now with a pencil, mark the straw 3.5cm (1⅜″) from each end.

Push the straw through the holes you punched so you have 3.5cm (1⅜″) sticking out from each end.

To keep the straw from pulling through, put sticky tape around the straw just under the 3.5cm (1⅜″) mark. Apply another sticky inside the 3.5cm (1⅜″) mark on the other side. (Temporarily elongate the cylindrical shape by squeezing it.)

Cut off a metre of nylon line and run it through the hollow straw.

Before going further, test to see that your UFO's in balance by holding each end of the bridle line and moving it up and down. The UFO should start spinning.

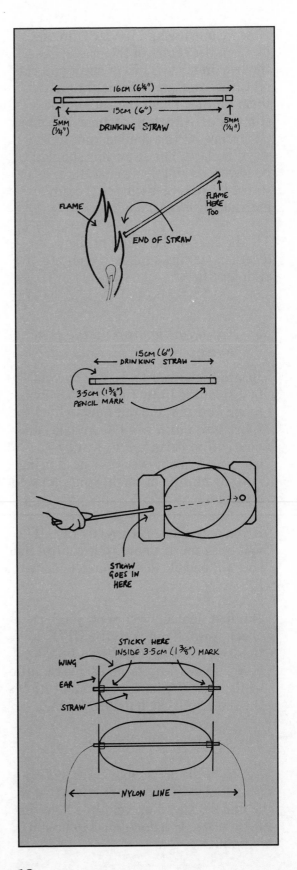

Now we must secure the UFO in one place on the centre of the bridle. Take the two 5mm (¼") bits of straw you cut off earlier and slip the line through them till they touch the ends of the straw axle. At that point, tie each 5mm (¼") straw bit in a double knot so it stays in place. The straw bits shouldn't be forced too tightly against the axle straw. Make sure 40cm (16") of line protrudes from each end.

Tie the ends of the nylon bridle together, making sure both ends are of even length.

▷ *Pre-flight testing inside your house*

Before you go out to fly, test fly your first spinning tinny right in your living room. You can find out how well it spins, how much wind it can take, and how well in balance it is, just by whirling it about over your head using nothing but the bridle in your hands to control it.

If you have made it correctly the UFO will be so much under your control that you will be able to do figure eights with it.

But first, like any test pilot, you have to check yourself out with the UFO. Remember the first time you tried a yo-yo, a hula hoop or bike? Took a little while to get the hang of it, didn't it? It's the same with the hand held UFO.

There's a trick, and this is it.

Lay the bridle across four fingers of one open hand with the centre knot right in the middle. Use your thumb to hold the line in place. You don't have to hold it too tight.

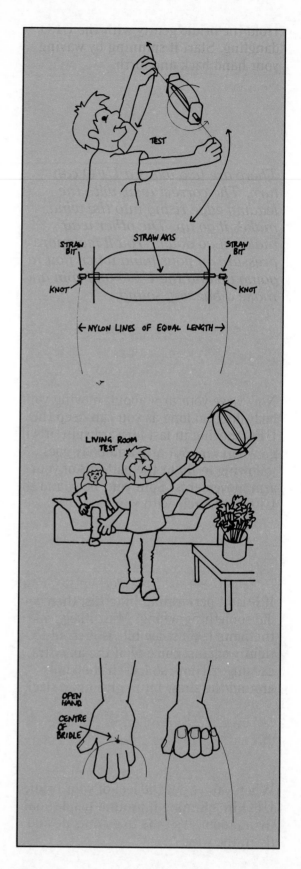

14

Hold the bridle gently with the UFO dangling. Start it spinning by waving your hand back and forth.

There are two ways a UFO can turn. The correct way, with the leading edge rising into the wind, makes it go up. The other way makes it go down. You'll feel more pressure on your hand when you're going up and the UFO will spin and make a buzzing sound.

Now wave your arm about, moving your body, too. So long as you can keep the UFO moving in fast forward spin, it will go wherever your arm and body goes, following in flight the patterns of your arm movements. Spin your body and the UFO will circle with you.

If it isn't performing like this, then you did something wrong. Most likely, one of the 5mm (¼″) straw bits is pressed too tightly against the end of the axle straw, causing friction, so loosen the knots around the straw bit to give more slack.

When you've got the feel of your bridled UFO by spinning it around inside your living room, it's time to go outside and fly in the wind.

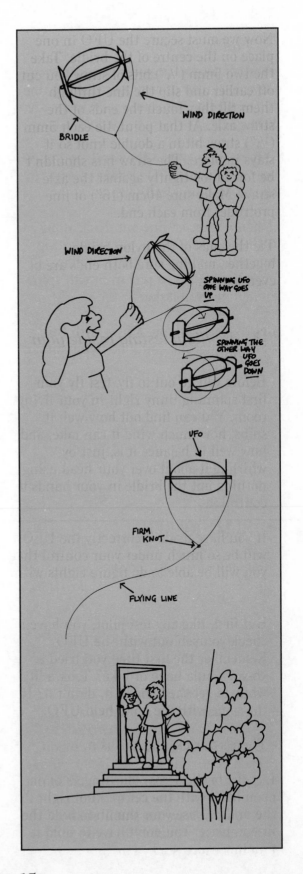

WIND DIRECTION

BRIDLE

WIND DIRECTION

SPINNING UFO ONE WAY GOES UP

SPINNING THE OTHER WAY UFO GOES DOWN

UFO

FIRM KNOT

FLYING LINE

▷ *Flying outside*

First, of course, tie your flying line (sewing thread or very light fishing line) to the bridle. Make sure your knots are firm.

When you're out in the wind, you need only hold your UFO up for the wind to start it spinning in flight.

When it flies, let line out. Ride along with the wind. When you stop letting line out and hold the UFO in place, it pulls harder. If you reel in, it will spin and climb even faster.

Get the feel of flying UFOs with this trainer. Later on, you'll be flying much bigger ones.

▶ BULL ROARER

What you will need:
- fibreglass rod 2mm (¹/₁₀″) diameter, 37.5cm (14¾″) long *(axle)*
- 2 pieces waterproof florists' ribbon, each 5cm x 40cm (2″ x 16″) *(wing)*
- 2 pieces waterproof florists' ribbon, each 5cm x 10cm (2″ x 4″) *(ears)*
- drinking straw, for small washers
- hat elastic, 1 metre (3′) long
- double-sided sticky tape

16

High Flyers

Prepare 'ears' by trimming corners and prepare fibreglass rod by marking in the centre (18.75cm (7⅜″) from each end) and again 17.5cm (7″) from each end.

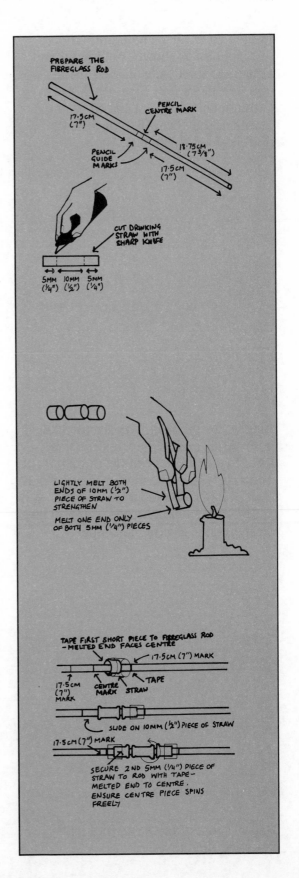

Using a very sharp knife, cut three washers from drinking straw. Make two 5mm (¼″) long and one 10mm (½″).

Using tweezers, lightly melt both ends of the 10mm (½″) piece to strengthen. Melt one end only on both 5mm (¼″) pieces.

Tape the first 5mm (¼″) piece to the fibreglass rod with the melted end facing the centre.

Slide on 10mm (½″) piece and then secure the second 5mm (¼″) piece with tape (melted end to the centre). Ensure centre piece spins freely.

Make first wing as in diagram and
punch holes as shown. Fold wing and
attach ear to outside of wing using
double-sided sticky tape. Push rod
through both holes in the wing and
secure at the 15cm (6″) mark with
double-sided sticky tape.

Before closing wing, tape around rod at
both inside ends. The wing must be
fixed to outside edge of tape holding the
5mm (¼″) straw washer in place. Then
close the wing by securing ends to
double-sided tape. Squeeze wing to give
both sections a rounded shape.

Repeat process for the second wing,
reversing directions.

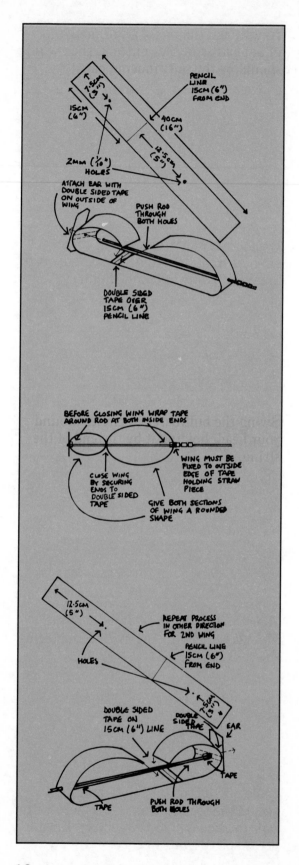

Now attach the metre (yard) long piece of hat elastic to the centre washer, which should be the only moving part.

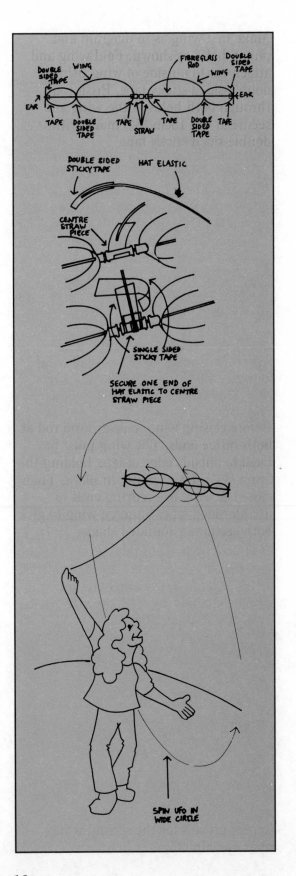

Swing the bullroarer in circles around your head, holding it by the end of the string.

High Flyers

To make large UFOs that fly hundreds of metres (yards) high, we need tougher materials. Ribbon and straws won't do. We need a waterproof synthetic film (Mylar is ideal, but the shiny metallic gift wrap available by the sheet works perfectly well), and fibreglass rods. The combination of these two materials will give you a flying object that will last.

For where to get what you need, see the list at the end of the book.

We'll start with the basic High Flyer UFO. It is made up of two flat ovoid pieces. One acts as a wing and it is bisected by the other, which acts as the ear.

Remember, there is a lot of tolerance in the sizes I give you and therefore lots of room for substitution and improvisation.

Using the techniques described here, but bigger and stronger materials, there is almost no limit to the size UFO you can make. For example, to make a UFO twice as large as the one here, just proportionately increase the size and strength of materials.

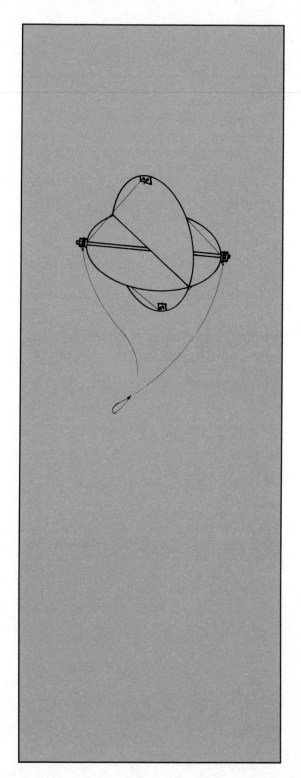

What you need:

- 2 pieces fibreglass rod 2mm ($^1/_{10}$″) diameter, each 1 metre (39$^1/_2$″) long
- fibreglass rod 4mm ($^3/_{20}$″) diameter, 45cm (17$^3/_4$″) long *(axle)*
- waterproof synthetic film, 50cm x 100cm (20″ x 40″)
- 2 pieces hollow plastic tube 4mm ($^3/_{20}$″) diameter, each 5cm (2″) long *(connectors)*
- 4 rubber washers, 2mm ($^1/_{10}$″) inner diameter
- 2 large fishing swivels (or other swivels)
- fishing line, 5kg (12lb) test, 1 metre (3′) long
- double-sided sticky tape, 12mm ($^1/_2$″) wide
- strong waterproof sticky tape
- hat elastic, 1.3 metres (4′3″) long
- ruler, pencil
- scissors or sharp blade

▶ HERE'S HOW YOU MAKE IT

▷ *The skeleton (frame)*

First, mark each large fibreglass rod at its exact centre (50cm (19$^3/_4$″) mark).

Take one of the large fibreglass rods and put a tiny piece of double-sided tape on each end. Then plug each end into a hollow plastic connector. Make into circles by joining their ends with the hollow plastic connectors.

Using about 27cm (10$^1/_2$″) of strong sticky tape, pull the circle into an oval shape by stretching the strong tape from the centre of the connector to the mark we made earlier on the rod. Make the distance across 22cm (8$^1/_2$″). Wrap tape securely on each end to make sure the shape remains.

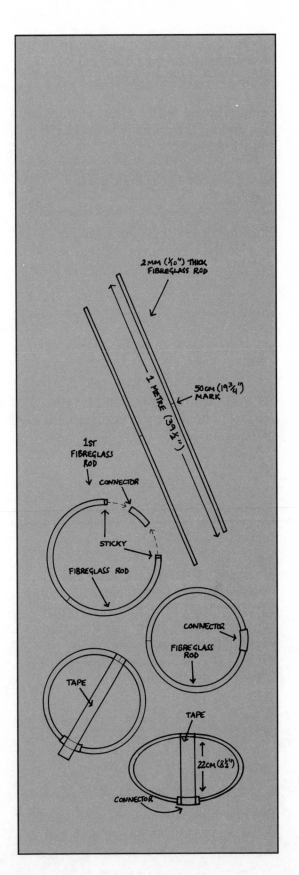

21

Lay the axle rod across the centre of the tape so that it extends 3.5cm (1⅜″) beyond each end of the wing.

Secure the rod to the wing by wrapping tape around the points where the rod and wing touch.

Now you have the complete wing skeleton.

Now for the ear skeleton, which is simpler. Take your other fibreglass rod and put a mark at exact centre as before.

As with the other one, bend it into a circle and hold the rod in place with the plastic connector.

Also, as with the other circle, make it into an oval by fitting a piece of *strong* tape from the connector to the centre mark on the rod. Only this time, the width of the oval *must be 24cm (9½″)*. This is because the wing will later slot into the ear.

You now have a wing skeleton and an ear skeleton. All we have to do is put a skin over them.

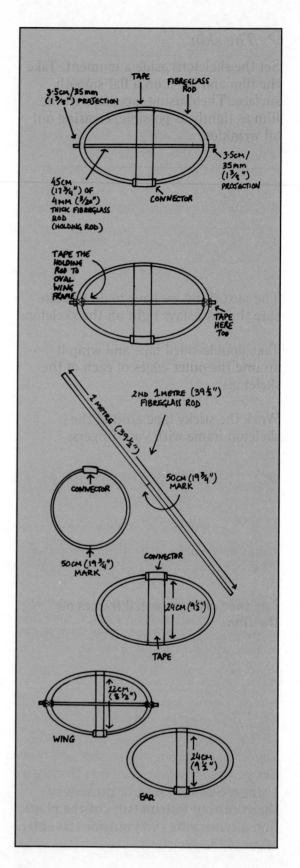

▷ *The skin*

Set the skeletons aside a moment. Take the film and lay it on a flat smooth surface. Then, using tape, stretch the film as tightly as possible, creasing out all wrinkles.

The next thing we have to do is make sure the skin stays tight on the skeleton.

Take double-sided tape and wrap it around the outer edges of each of the skeletons.

Work the sticky tape around the skeleton frame with your fingers.

Lay the two tape-coated frames on the film.

Using a Stanley knife, or other very sharp cutting instrument, cut the plastic film a centimetre (½″) outside the outer edges of the skeletons.

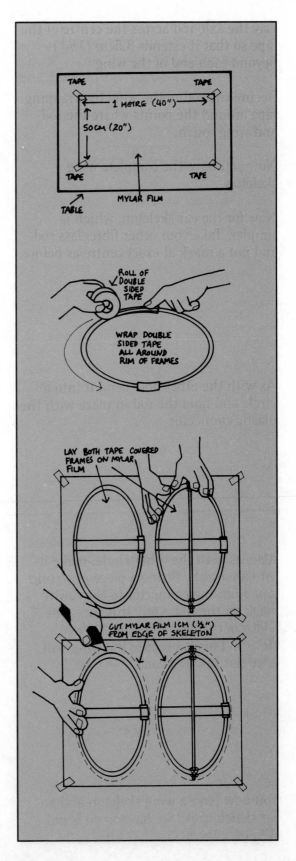

23

Now roll this overlap around the fibreglass so it completely covers the adhesive and no fibreglass can be seen. To do this, work gently with thumb and forefinger from one end to the other. (You're reinforcing the grip of the sticky tape on both skeleton and skin.)

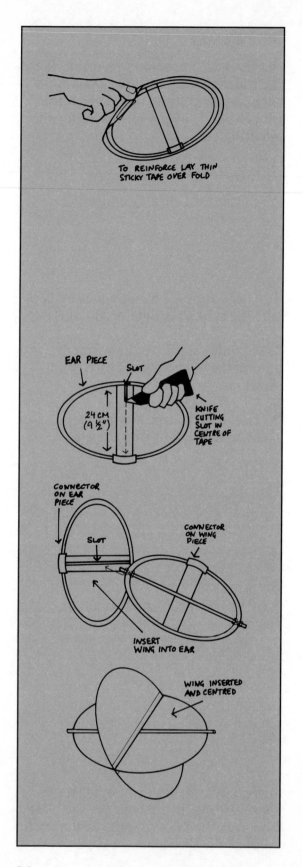

TO REINFORCE LAY THIN STICKY TAPE OVER FOLD

EAR PIECE
SLOT
24 CM (9½")
KNIFE CUTTING SLOT IN CENTRE OF TAPE

CONNECTOR ON EAR PIECE
SLOT
CONNECTOR ON WING PIECE
INSERT WING INTO EAR

WING INSERTED AND CENTRED

▷ *Assembly*

Take the ear piece (24cm (9½″) wide) and cut a slot down the exact middle of the tape that's holding it in shape.

We're going to insert the wing through the ear slot. But first, to keep it in balance, *make sure the plastic connectors,* which are added weight, are on opposite sides.

Insert the 22cm (8½″) wide wing through the slot so that it is exactly centred.

Now we secure the wing in place right in the centre. Let it lie flat on its ear. Apply strong sticky tape across both wing and ear where they touch.

Apply the strong sticky tape on all four sides where the wing and the ear touch each other.

Now you have the basic high flying UFO. There are just two more things we have to do: make the ears stand up automatically from a flat position, and then bridle it.

First, the automatically rising ears. Cut two pieces of hat elastic each 64cm (25½″) long. Tie the centre of each piece to the outer edge of the wing where it touches the axle with a firm double knot.

Now we have four loose ends we'll be tying to the top of the ears. Before we tie, we have to pierce holes through the ear's skin for the elastic to go through.

But before we do that, we're going to reinforce the spot to be pierced with a piece of strong tape.

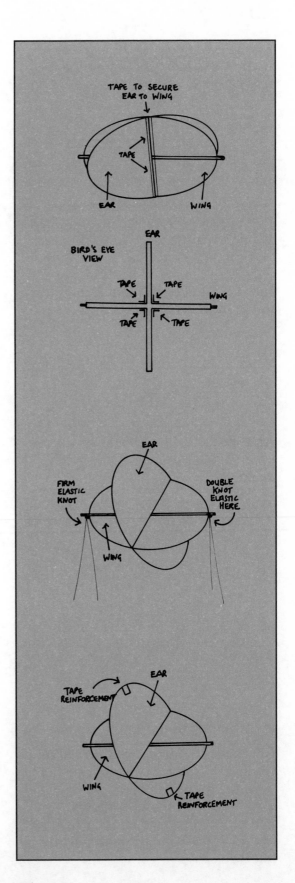

25

Punch two tiny holes through the ear where it's reinforced. Two on the top and two on the bottom.

Now take the loose elastic lines and run them up through the holes, and when the pull is just enough to hold the ear vertical (that is, at right angles to the wing), tie a couple of knots on the end of the elastic to keep it from slipping back out of the hole.

All four elastic lines should now be evenly stretched and the ear at right angles to the wing.

▷ *The bridle*

Now for the bridle. First, to make sure the axle doesn't break loose from the wing in a strong wind, wrap a couple of turns of tape on the axle where it touches the wing and on the wing itself, just as a back-up to the tape you already put there.

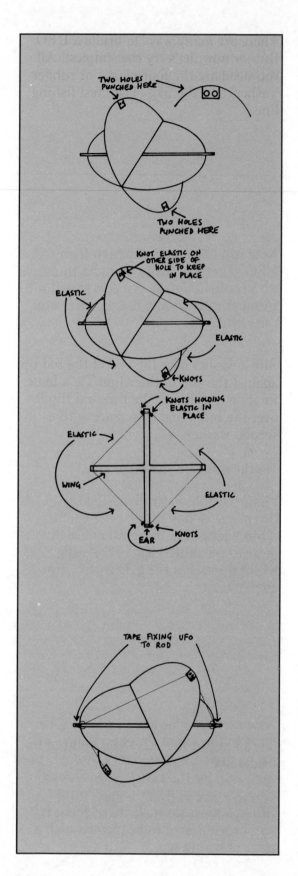

26

There are many ways to bridle a UFO. But for now, let's try the simplest. All you need are the four plastic or rubber washers and the 5kg (12lb) test fishing line.

Slip a washer over the end of the rod up against the end of the wing. Tie a loose knot on one end of the line and slip it over the rod. Hold it in place with a second washer.

Do the same on the other side.

Tie a knot in the exact mid point of the bridle line.

You're ready to fly. Use 5kg (12lb) test lines, preferably on the end of a fishing rod, and it will climb as high as you let it go.

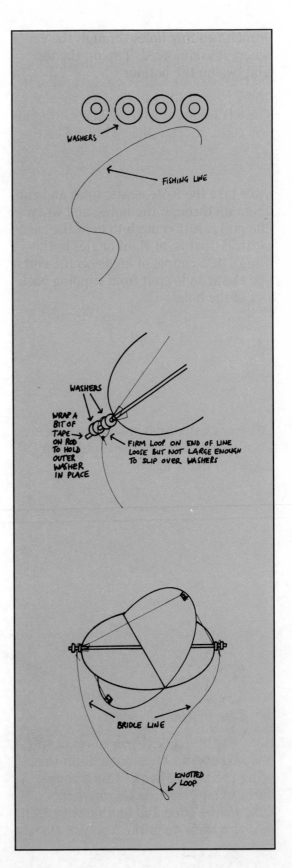

WASHERS

FISHING LINE

WASHERS

WRAP A BIT OF TAPE ON ROD TO HOLD OUTER WASHER IN PLACE

FIRM LOOP ON END OF LINE LOOSE BUT NOT LARGE ENOUGH TO SLIP OVER WASHERS

BRIDLE LINE

KNOTTED LOOP

If your UFO doesn't fly squarely, it can be corrected by adjusting the bridle. If the UFO is tilting to the left, shorten the left bridle. If your UFO is tilting to the right, shorten the right bridle.

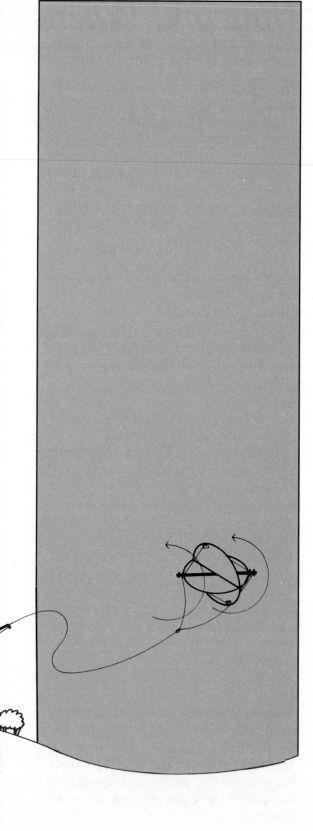

How and Where to Fly

The biggest difference between a UFO
and other flying things is its versatility.
It can fly from places where ordinary
kites cannot fly. In fact there are few
places where a UFO cannot fly. Once
you capture that feel of knowing when
to reel in and when to let line out, you
can guide your UFO anywhere, from
centimetres above an ocean wave to the
tip of a clock tower.

I cannot over-emphasise how much
more fun it is to fly a UFO with a
fishing rod and reel.

- You launch it with a flick of the wrist
  and you control altitude.

- Let line out and the UFO drops.

- Reel line in and the UFO climbs.

Whenever you fly a UFO, you're playing
a hide-and-seek game with the wind. It's
up to you to find the best places to fly.
Bridges, roofs, balconies, boats and
bicycles.

After you have been flying your UFO a
while, you will learn to tell from the feel
of the wind on your face what lifting
power it will give. When the wind is
very light, walk forward into the breeze
and feel it on your face. There's a certain
pressure that tells you it's enough to
give lift.

And every so often look behind you to
see what kind of wind is coming. Are
those trees in the distance bending their
top branches? Is the grass behind you
moving? Are things blowing about on
the ground? Keep an eye on flags and
smoke from a chimney.

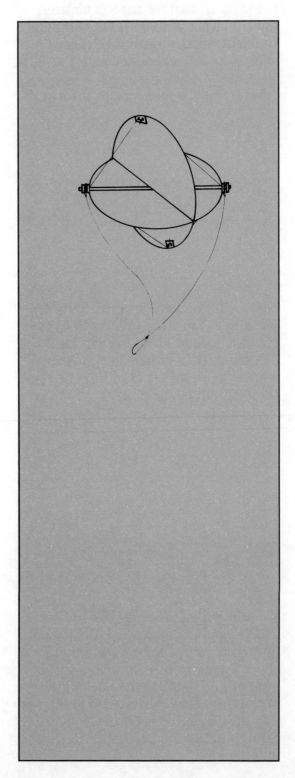

29

▶ FLYING IN A PARK OR A PADDOCK

If you're in a paddock, go to the end of the paddock that the wind is blowing towards. That way you're farthest away from structures which might block the wind, such as trees or houses.

Always fly with your back to the wind.

Never walk backwards or run with it like a kite. Too often you run away from the clear area to where the wind is blocked by trees or buildings. If the wind is right, the UFO will fly with you standing still in one place.

If you're without fishing gear and the wind is too light to let the UFO launch from your hand, lay it on the ground about 7 to 10 metres (20 to 30 feet) in front of you, then tug the line. With practice you'll be able to get it to flip up into the breeze. Or have somebody throw it in the air, giving it its first spin into the wind.

▶ FLYING FROM A BRIDGE

A bridge is an ideal place to fly. Drop your UFO over the down wind side of the bridge. Let the UFO catch the air current under the bridge and start spinning. Let the wind carry it out across the water until it's far enough away to be clear of the downwind turbulence. Reel in slightly, and it will start to climb.

From a bridge, you can be at a higher altitude than the UFO you're flying and that lets you have much more room to do tricks. Let it drop to within inches of the water below and then by reeling in quickly shoot it straight up hundreds of feet high. There are strange wind currents and eddies.

Let me describe my experiences flying from London's Waterloo Bridge. My UFO flashes high above lighted skyscrapers and can be seen all over town. And I'm safe flying from a bridge because I've got plenty of water to manoeuvre over without having to worry about cars and dogs and people and trees.

From Waterloo Bridge, the UFO can tap the windows of the upper floors of the Savoy Hotel and hover inches from the clock on the spotlighted Shell Mex building. Or I can make my UFO swoop down to divebomb passing boats.

Be prepared for some strange wind currents along rivers. The different temperatures between water and land can do tricky things with the breezes which cross them. The UFO may loop and dive and go wherever the wind takes it, but it will still be up there when the wind settles.

When flying from a bridge, watch out for boats passing beneath you. Make sure when you drop your UFO over the side there's no river traffic below. Also, don't fly if the wind puts your UFO over a road.

There will come a time when due to bad judgement the UFO will drop in the water. Just reel it in slowly so as not to put too much pressure on the line and the UFO will surface and leap back into the air.

▶ FLYING FROM A BOAT

If you're on a small boat, choose a spot where you feel the breeze coming towards you and then launch the UFO. Usually that's at the front of the craft, but it doesn't have to be. I've flown from the rear decks of ferries. As when flying from a bridge, you can drop your UFO to the water and then zoom upwards. You can bring it to within a metre (3') of you and then let it go.

It's a whole new experience. Flying from a motorboat leaves you independent of the wind. The forward motion of the boat makes the UFO spin and take flight and it will stay on course even if the boat travels in circles.

Make sure your line's strong enough to handle a speeding boat.

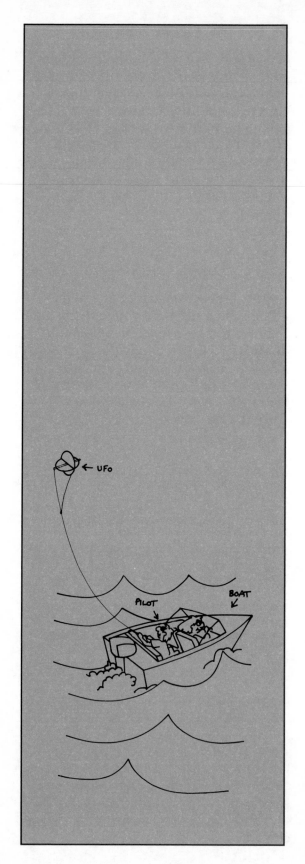

Bull Roarer and Spinning Tinnys

UFO Gliders

▶ FLYING FROM A BICYCLE

The way to fly a UFO from a bicycle is to tie it on top of a vertical rod attached to the rear of the bike. (Some shops sell rods made of fibreglass with a small flag on top for putting on a bike.) Tie or tape the UFO to the top of the pole, using only 20cm (8″) of lead line. Once you start pedalling, the UFO will start spinning and it will lift itself above the pole.

▶ FLYING FROM A ROOF

Flying a UFO from a roof has great advantages, especially if the roof is higher than surrounding buildings. Any time you can fly the UFO below the height at which you're standing, you have a lot more control. This assumes you're using a fishing rod and reel or kite reel. You can drop down to within centimetres (inches) of lower roof tops and you have a big margin for error.

Even if the UFO goes into a spin because of the tricky winds you find among buildings, it can safely be put right by reeling in quickly. *Make sure to keep it away from trees and other obstructions that could snare it. Never allow the UFO to be in a position where it might drop on the road or distract drivers.*

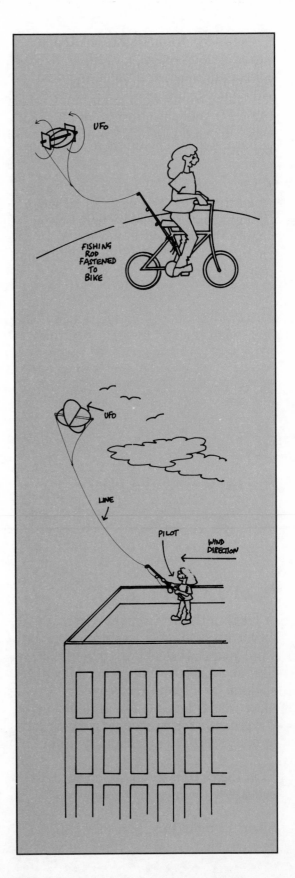

▶ FLYING IN THE MOUNTAINS

My favourite UFO flight is over mountains. There's nothing like launching from a high mountain so that the UFO goes down instead of up. That way you can fly over valleys and trees beneath you.

Always keep a UFO and reel in the car when travelling. You never know when it might come in handy. There's even a chance that if you're lost or in an emergency, the UFO will be sighted and help will arrive!

▶ UFO NIGHT FLIGHTS

A UFO in the sky at night reflects the city lights below. It's a spinning mirror. Find an area that's lit up. It could be an illuminated historic building, a floodlit stadium, or a spotlit rock concert. Any place where there are lots of lights on the ground. You need a big parking lot or open space to launch and fly from.

Find the right place to fly so your UFO gets above the most lighted spots.

Since it's night time, your line will be invisible.

▶ WHERE NOT TO FLY

- *Never* fly over high tension wires.

- *Never* fly close to airports.

- *Never* fly in thunderstorms.

- *Never* fly in any situation where your UFO may come down on a busy road.

- *Never* fly where your UFO may distract drivers.

- Find out your local laws about flying a 'thing on a string', and stay within them.

▶ WIND AND WEATHER

Wherever you fly, the wind can be either your partner or your enemy. Get to know it well. Either you work with it, or it works against you. Both you and the wind contribute to the turning speed of the UFO. When you're just holding the line without reeling it in or out, the wind does all the turning. If you want to make the UFO turn faster and climb higher, reel line in quickly to speed up the rotation of the UFO. You want it to drop? Let line out to slow the rotation of the UFO.

The best winds to fly in are the gentlest ones, around 10-15kph (6-10mph). With these gentle winds I control the spin speed as much as the wind. In strong winds, above 30kph (20mph), the wind is in control. In very high winds my UFO will go into aerobatics, diving, doing loops and pulling hard on the line. I have to know when to take advantage of drops in wind speed to reel in, and how to let out line to ride out sudden gusts, to take the strain off my line. I'm like a sailor in a small sailboat on heavy seas.

Try to find unusual wind currents and ride them. It could be a wind going up a valley. It could be a breeze striking a cliff and rising upwards. It could be a wind coming from a lake or ocean shore. The most fun breeze of all to ride is a thermal. When you catch one of these your UFO is lifted almost straight upwards, sometimes with the line completely slack, with no pull on it whatsoever.

36

▷ *Finding a thermal*

How do you find a thermal? This is
what a glider pilot once told me. Wait
for a day of blue sky studded with white
cumulus clouds; a day when the ground
breeze is gentle. Look up in the sky and
you'll see a row of white clouds in line,
receding into the distance. If you get in
line with those clouds right above you,
you're in thermal country.

Another way is to spot birds overhead
riding thermals. When you see a flock
floating all together in a small area
without flapping their wings, gulls
especially, they're having fun on
a thermal.

UFO Novelties

The great things about UFOs is that you don't have to fly to have fun with them. You can make small ones which spin over your head as part of a hat. You can make them into garden decorations which spin and flash light, day and night. They are easily rigged to spin as ornaments inside the house. You can hang them on verandahs, balconies, rooftops and even trees. You can string dozens of them side by side so they're all spinning on a single line.

Let's start with UFO headgear.

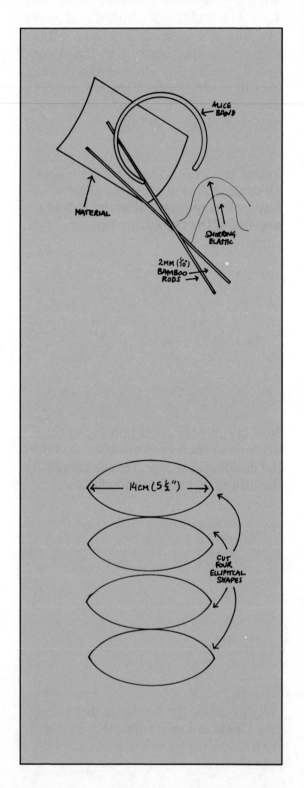

▶ UFO HEADGEAR

What you need:
- 2 pieces bamboo rod, 2mm (1/10″) thick (or plastic, wire, or fibreglass), each 36cm (14″) long
- material (synthetic film, paper, cardboard), 20cm x 14cm (8″ x 5½″)
- plastic head band (Alice band, the sort that goes over the top of your head and clasps behind your ears)
- 2 pieces shirring elastic, each 12cm (5″) long
- double-sided sticky tape
- sticky tape

Two very small UFOs spin from this headgear. Cut four elliptical shapes out of the material. Since this UFO is not for flying, weight is not such a factor so you can make them from paper if nothing else is available. Each shape should look like the diagram.

Take one of these cutouts and on each pointed end apply about one square centimetre (½ square inch) of double-sided tape.

Lay a piece of elastic shirring thread on one end of the cutout.

Now lay another cutout on top of this first one so their ends are both sealed by the double-sided tape. Do the same with the other two cutouts and elastic.

Now we make the headgear that these two UFOs can spin from. We do this with the Alice band hairclasp and the flexible rods.

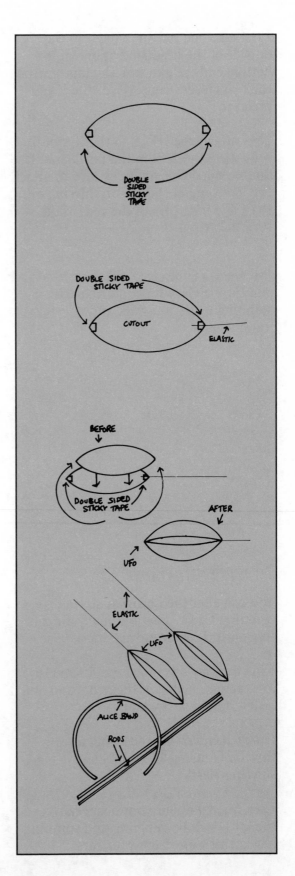

First take one rod and tape it to the outside of the headband at one of its bottom ends. Make sure the tape grasps the two pieces firmly. (Use glue if you prefer it.)

Now attach the UFOs to the tips of the rods sticking up from the headband. Use double-sided tape or sticky tape to attach the loose end of the elastic shirring on the UFO to the tip of the rod. Make sure the grip is firm.

Put the UFO headgear on your head and the UFOs will dangle above it, spinning while you walk and move about.

▷ *UFO 'Earrings'*

You can alter the headgear so the spinning UFOs dangle below your ears like gigantic spinning earrings.

This time lay a bamboo rod 40cm (16″) long across the top of the headband and fasten it with sticky tape.

On each end of the rod, hang a tiny UFO, using 12cm (5″) of shirring elastic.

Now when you put your headgear on, the UFO will be dangling and spinning just inches away from your ears.

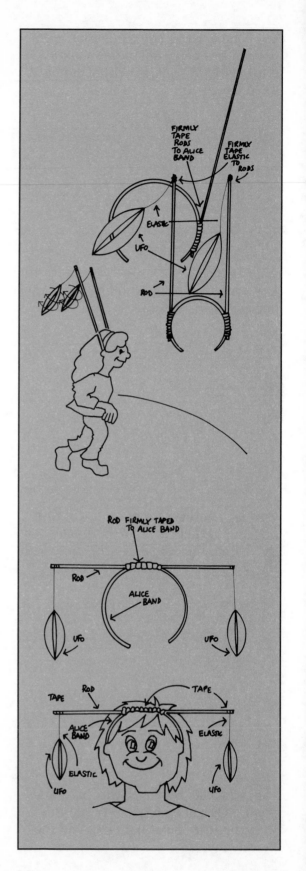

▷ *Feather UFO*

The simplest UFO hat you can make is to take a long feather and tie a tiny UFO on a piece of thin elastic shirring thread to the feather tip.

Then stick the feather in your hat. The UFO will dangle from the tip of the feather and spin right over your head.

▶ CYLINDRICAL UFO

Before we leave hats, there is one other design that's very effective, both on hats and in other decorative functions. This is a perfectly cylindrical UFO.

Cut out a piece of material (florists' ribbon paper), 6cm x 24cm (2½″ x 9½″).

Seal the ends of the material together with sticky tape and you have a cylindrical UFO.

Attach about 8cm (3″) of elastic line to the centre of the cylinder.

The cylinder shape makes the inside of the UFO more visible and increases the artistic effect.

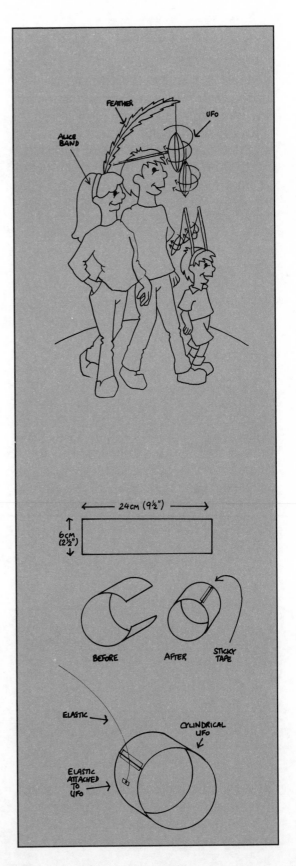

▶ UFO DECORATIONS FOR OUTSIDE

Cut out slightly larger elliptical (or cylindrical) UFOs and hang them about the house, garden, verandah or roof. They'll spin day and night in the slightest air currents and will withstand quite strong ones. When lights shine on them, they're spectacular.

Make the decorative UFO like you made the hat UFOs, using two elliptical shapes pressed against each other and fastened on each end. Use a 20cm (8″) long elliptical shape and a 15cm (6″) piece of shirring elastic.

Tape the free end of the shirring elastic to wherever you want to tie it; maybe the ceiling, a light fixture, or over a doorway like you'd hang mistletoe.

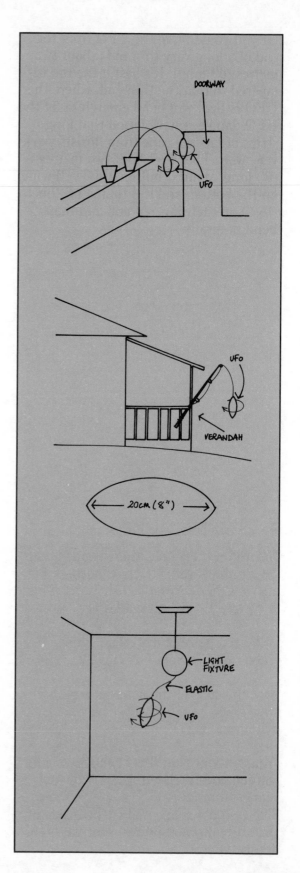

Or you could hang the UFO from the end of a long very thin rod (about two metres (6') long). It's best if the rod is tapered so that the thin end, where the UFO is tied, will bend enough to let the UFO dangle. I have found that long strips of tapered cane from florists work very well. They are about two metres (6') long, about 5 millimetres (1/4") wide on the bottom and less than a millimetre (1/20") on their tapered end and they bend naturally.

You can just plant the rod in your garden and the UFO will dangle and start spinning.

You can also hang it out your window like a flag.

43

Remember, the elliptical and cylindrical shapes are only two of many which can be used for decorations. Think up your own designs. You'll be surprised how many different shapes will work.

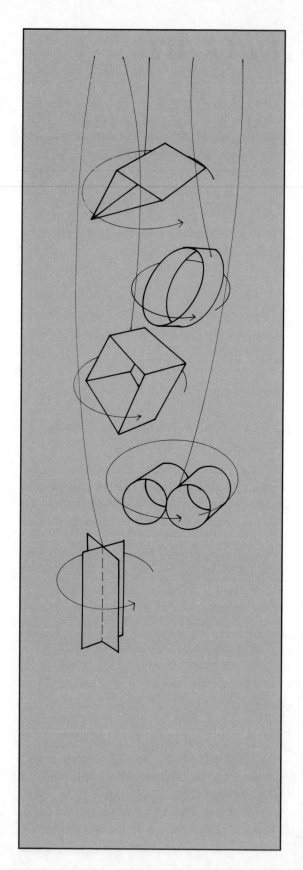

UFO Art

I have a lot of fun just decorating UFOs and seeing what my decorations look like when they're spinning.

Let's practice this spinning art using UFO gliders and coloured marker pens. Or you might like to try using metallic sticky tapes now available.

It's best to do artwork before assembly. It's easier to draw on a flat surface than a curved one, as any Michaelangelo will tell you.

First, the Double X effect. On the upper side of the UFO glider, draw two diagonal lines across the wing, going from top left to bottom right.

Turn the glider over. This time draw two diagonal lines exactly in line with the ones on top. That means drawing them from bottom left to top right. If you did it right, the diagonal lines on the upper side of the glider are exactly on top of the diagonal lines on the underside of the glider.

Flip the UFO in the air and you'll notice that when it spins the diagonal lines criss cross, so what you see are two crosses wiggling back and forth.

Try other lines. Draw triangles and circles in different colours on both sides of the glider and watch them 'move' when the glider starts spinning. You get a good effect if you just stipple red and blue and green and yellow dots on both sides of the glider.

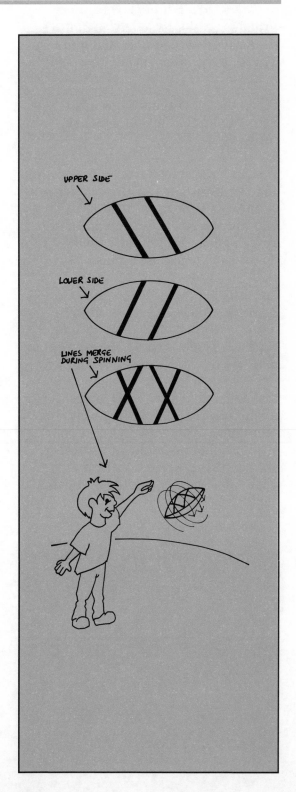

UPPER SIDE

LOWER SIDE

LINES MERGE DURING SPINNING

You can put messages on your UFO too; your name perhaps. Just put one word on one side in red and another word on the other side in blue. For example, write in the biggest letters possible the word 'UFO' on one side. Again in big letters on the other side write 'SAM'.

When the UFO spins the words UFO-Sam-UFO-Sam hit your eyes like a strobe light.

We can make it look like an eye opening and closing as it spins. Use marker pens or any colouring agent that doesn't eat into the plastic. Draw open and shut eyes on all surfaces of the cylinders, so that the eye winks as it spins.

Try using all four sides of your 2-cylinder model. Eyeballs on the inside, eyebrows and lashes on the outside. Make it so only one eye winks as it spins.

One last note. Every UFO glider you colour and design is a unique form of spinning art. You will find, as I did, great delight and fascination in every one you make, because you won't know what you've 'painted' until you see it spinning.

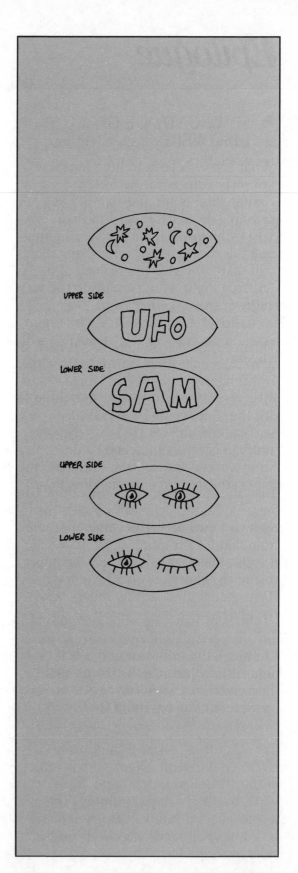

UPPER SIDE

LOWER SIDE

UPPER SIDE

LOWER SIDE

Epilogue

▶ MY UFO VOYAGE OF DISCOVERY

What I have been searching for these last forty years is the perfect combination of lift and stability in a spinning device. By that I mean a UFO which will fly in the very lightest and the very strongest winds, one that will soar to heights undreamed of in tethered flight, even perhaps to the very edges of space.

When I started flying my UFOs back in 1947, the only wing known to fly while spinning was an S-shaped wing. Everybody thought that for the thing to fly, the wind would have to hit a curved surface and turn it. That was the case until 1977 when I discovered that a flat wing worked better. To my surprise, the UFO still spun in only one direction.

I started playing with combinations of round and flat shapes, and I made a startling discovery. It doesn't really matter what kind of shape the wing is.

If you spin something light enough in an airstream, it will fly steadily so long as there's the right balance of horizontal and vertical features. Anything that's horizontal in a spinning device will provide lift and anything that's vertical will provide stability. A shape that's curved or at an angle will provide both lift and stability.

I made more than a hundred different shaped UFOs before I discovered that lift and stability come as much from spin as from the shape of an object.

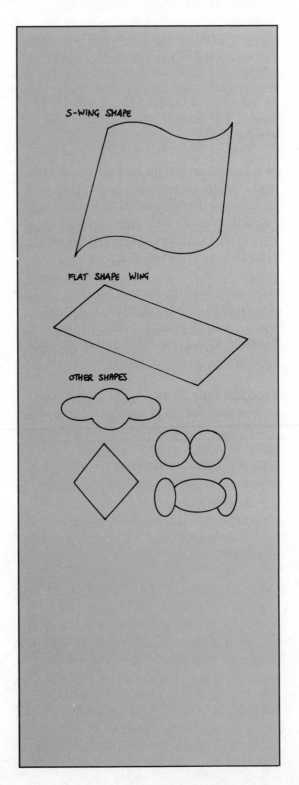

S-WING SHAPE

FLAT SHAPE WING

OTHER SHAPES

Weight, of course, is important to lift. When you add weight to a UFO, you normally reduce its lift … but not always. One surprising exception is when you put 'ears' on the end of a curved cylindrical or oval shaped wing. Ears create extra stability, and this confers lift which more than compensates for the added weight.

▶ WHAT MAKES A UFO FLY?

It was purest coincidence that my discovery of what makes a UFO fly coincided with the writing of this book. Over the years I had asked far and wide for explanations of their flight and it was only recently that I received a letter from Lee Spector, a physicist in Seattle, USA. His explanation makes more sense than any I've heard in forty years of flying spinning things. It seems that the UFOs we're making are on the cutting edge of aeronautical discovery.

Lee Spector says that what makes the UFO spin and create lift are miniature *horizontal tornadoes* emanating from the UFO's wingtips. These same *vortices* occur with airplanes. On jet planes they can stretch out five miles (eight kilometres) and they're so powerful on a jet that light planes too close to them can be knocked out of the sky.

With a spinning wing, the vortex effect is greater. Once the UFO starts spinning, the air on top goes down and the air underneath goes up, and together they spin over and around the UFO, narrowing at the wingtips, where the spinning is fastest and then expanding backwards. The UFO is spinning between the narrow ends of two horizontal tornadoes; in effect, it's like spinning between the tornadoes' fingers.

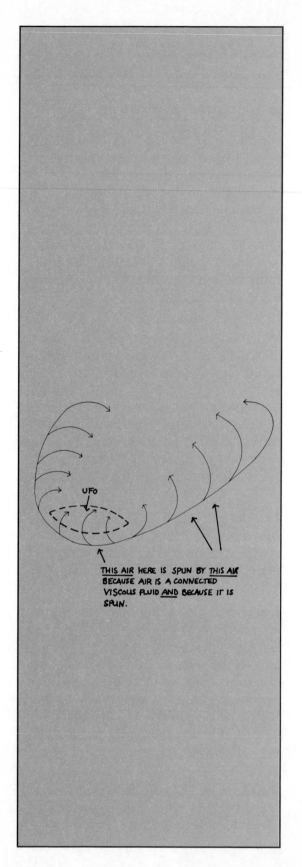

UFO

THIS AIR HERE IS SPUN BY THIS AIR BECAUSE AIR IS A CONNECTED VISCOUS FLUID AND BECAUSE IT IS SPUN.

Useful Information

▶ **SOME TERMS**

Axle The central axis on which the UFO spins. Usually a rod or straw.

Bridle The double line that attaches the UFO to the single line string in your hand. Some bridles are rigid (U-shaped), some are flexible (V-shaped).

Ears Any part of a UFO sticking upwards. Ears give it stability.

Hollow Axle Bridle A bridle made with a drinking straw.

Rod The axle rod. Often hollow.

Wing Any part of a UFO reaching outward. Wings give it lift.

In some designs it's hard to tell where the ears end and the wings begin. In cylindrical UFOs, ears and wings are merged.

▶ **MATERIALS**

Elastic Hat elastic is great for whirling a small UFO around your head indoors.

Shirring elastic is almost as fine as thread and it is bought by the reel. Buy it in fabric and sewing shops.

Fabrics Mylar, synthetic film, rip-stop nylon. See individual entries.

Fibreglass rod 2mm ($1/10"$) and 4mm ($3/20"$) diameter. Buy in kite stores.

Double-sided sticky tape This is similar to sticky tape, except it is sticky on both sides. Available at stationers and supermarkets. See also 'sticky pads'.

Fishing line Nylon is essential for bridles and the main flying line. Small UFOs will fly on line as light as 1kg (2lb) test. Larger UFOs may need 5kg (10lb), 10kg (20lb) or in exceptional cases, 25kg (50lb) test.

Glue Quick drying waterproof superglue is best. Use glue as a backup to tape. *Test glue first in case it harms the materials you're using.*

Marker pens For decorating foam plastic UFOs. *Some brands eat right through foam plastic, so test them first.*

Mylar An exceptionally strong and light plastic film. It is more expensive than other plastic films. Available from some kite shops in clear or metallic forms.

'Mylar' is also a term used for synthetic film gift wraps which make an excellent substitute.

Plastic film Mylar is the best (see separate entry). Other plastic films are cheaper and work fine, but they tear more easily.

Rip-stop fabric This nylon fabric can be used instead of Mylar on advanced UFOs. It has to be sewn in place as it won't take glue or tape.

Rods Can be made of a variety of materials, including drinking straws, hollow plastic, fibreglass, cane, and carbon fibre (extra strong but expensive).

50

Sticky pads Double-sided 'stickies' are available from stationers, newsagents, etc. 'Mounting Squares' (from 3M) are suitable and double-sided tape is also available by the roll. 1.5mm (1/20″) thickness is fine.

Straws Drinking straws come in many sizes. The larger the diameter, the greater the strength.

String Keep it light and strong and water repellant.

Synthetic film gift wraps These are available in over 100 colours and designs and make an excellent substitute for Mylar. They can be obtained in sheet and roll form from gift shops and major department stores.

Swivels Fishing swivels can be used to connect the ends of the axle to the bridle of large high flying UFOs. Keep them light.

Tape Tape should be strong and stick perfectly when wet. Don't forget about double-sided tape. The best and strongest tape is strapping tape with fibreglass hairs in it.

Coloured tape is great for decorating UFOs, but take into account the added weight.

Washers Rubber or plastic.

> REMEMBER: Keep everything as light as can be.
> Keep everything fastened as tight as can be.

▶ WHERE TO BUY MATERIALS

Fishing shops — fishing rods, reels, nylon lines, swivels.

Garden centres — cane rods and waterproof florists ribbon.

Gift shops — waterproof synthetic film. Large department stores usually have a good gift wrap department.

Hardware shops — washers, string.

Hobby shops — rods.

Kite shops — reels, rods, Mylar, fabrics, string.

Sewing shops — Shirring and hat elastic.

▶ TOOLS

Blades should be razor sharp (eg Stanley knife), so take care.

Compass for drawing perfect circles.

Hack saw to cut rods.

Hole punch

Pliers

Ruler for straight lines and accuracy in measurement.

Scissors

Square gets those angles perfect.

Stapler